teddy bear hamsters

by mervin f. roberts

Frontispiece:
A young male ruby-eyed, black-eared white Teddy Bear hamster.

Photographs not otherwise credited specifically in their captions were made by:

John Hall---pages 1, 4, 8, 9, 28, 29, 33, 34, 36, 37, 38, 43, 44, 45, 51, 55, 57, 60, 61, 62, 63, 64, 65, 68, 69, 72, 73, 81, 85, 89, 96

D.G. Robinson, Jr.---page 13, top

Roy Robonson---page 84

Mervin F. Roberts---pages 11, 15, 16, 17, 18, 20, 24, 25, 26, 27, 30, 31, 32, 66, 70, 75, 77, 94

Thigpen Photography---pages 50, 78

Louise Van der Meid---pages 12, 19, 22, 23, 40, 41, 42, 93

Distributed in the U.S.A. by T.F.H. Publications, Inc., 211 West Sylvania Avenue, P.O. Box 27, Neptune City, N.J. 07753; in England by T.F.H. (Gt. Britain) Ltd., 13 Nutley Lane, Reigate, Surrey; in Canada to the book store and library trade by Clarke, Irwin & Company, Clarwin House, 791 St. Clair Avenue West, Toronto 10, Ontario; in Canada to the pet trade by Rolf C. Hagen Ltd., 3225 Sartelon Street, Montreal 382, Quebec; in Southeast Asia by Y.W. Ong, 9 Lorong 36 Geylang, Singapore 14; in Australia and the south Pacific by Pet Imports Pty. Ltd., P.O. Box 149, Brookvale 2100, N.S.W., Australia. Published by T.F.H. Publications, Inc. Ltd., The British Crown Colony of Hong Kong. Printed in Hong Kong.

CONTENTS

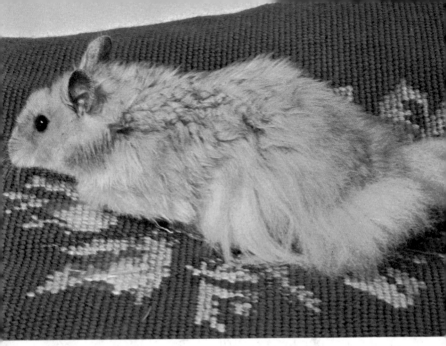

The two hamsters shown on this page could have been litter-mates. They are the same under the skin, but the Teddy Bear Hamster (above) looks very different from the shorthaired hamster below.

INTRODUCTION

In 1955, Dr. Herbert R. Axelrod, President of TFH Publications, asked me to illustrate a small hamster booklet which had been written by editors of his publishing company. Entitled "Hamsters as Pets," it gained a wide audience and several million copies were sold. Three years later he again called on me, this time to write and illustrate "How to Raise and Train a Pet Hamster." This was a larger booklet with natural color photos inside, and by then my family and I were strong admirers of pet hamsters. We even kept them when there was no book in preparation. Since 1958, the children I used as models have grown up, and a new outstanding variety of hamster has been established. Also, we have learned a lot more about hamsters over the course of those years. That is why this book was written. It is not just a new edition, but rather a complete revision and enlargement of the earlier versions with special emphasis on this new man-made hamster variety, the long-haired Teddy Bear. This hamster does not, and never did, exist in nature!

The genetics section is entirely new and should provide both answers and challenges to breeders and pet keepers. It was written by Dr. C. William Nixon, a professional geneticist of Randolph, Massachusetts, especially for this book and it contains information not otherwise readily available. Dr. Nixon has studied the history of the golden hamster in captivity. It began in 1930 when the first hamsters were caught near Aleppo, Syria and taken from there to Hebrew University in Israel where it was found that they would breed well under laboratory conditions. From Israel, some were sent to England and later to the U.S. Descendants of these first captive animals have spread far and wide and undoubtedly have totalled many hundreds of millions of animals in the ensuing forty plus years. It is most interesting that no further collections were made of wild specimens until the summer of 1971, when twelve more were collected in Syria and brought to the United States. These new animals are presently being carefully studied by Dr. Nixon in an effort to discover if differences exist between the two basic populations now in captivity—one having been in captivity for over forty years (in cages and under artificial conditions), the other representing the wild golden hamster population found in Syria today.

The sections on breeding and caging also present much new material which relates hamster habits to suggestions for care. Hopefully, this will reduce your effort, and increase your enjoyment.

The author thanks his wife for her thoughtful review and typing; Dr. Herbert R. Axelrod for his patience; Mr. Richard Smith of Stonehill Farms, Groton, Connecticut for his advice and the use of his animals; Dr. Nixon for his considerable and thoughtful effort; and Mr. John G. Hall of Old Saybrook, Connecticut for photographs.

MERVIN F. ROBERTS
Old Lyme, Connecticut

1.

HAMSTER FACTS

Maximum Age	Approximately 1000 days
Life Expectancy	$1\frac{1}{2}$ years
Breeding Age, Minimum	Female—$1\frac{1}{2}$ to 2 months
	Male—$3\frac{1}{2}$ to 4 months
Age at Puberty	Female—30 days
	Male—60 days
Polyestrous Circle	4 days
Gestation Period	16 to 19 days
Weaning Age	21 days
Temperature, Rectal	97.2° F to 99.5° F range
Respiratory Rate★	74 breaths/min., average
	33 minimum, 127 maximum
Rate of Heartbeat★	380-412 beats/min.
Food Consumption, Daily	10-15 grams
Water Consumption, Daily	15-20 milliliters
Urinary Volume, Daily	Up to 12 milliliters

★ Respiration and heartbeat during normal activity as above, but greatly reduce during aestivation and hibernation.

Ruby-eyed, dark-eared white young male Teddy Bear hamster. Compare this male with the female on the facing page. This difference is typical of Teddy Bear hamsters today. The male has longer hair, but both sexes have the soft fuzzy hair not seen in a normal shorthaired hamster.

Ruby-eyed pink-eared white young female Teddy Bear hamster, just barely old enough to breed. Teddy Bear Hamsters are also known as and sold under the name of "Hippie" hamsters.

2.

THE LONG-HAIRED TEDDY BEAR HAMSTER

The golden hamster was first described in 1839 by Waterhouse and he named it *Cricetus (Mesocricetus) auratus.*

meso = middle-sized (from the Greek)
cricetus = hamster (from the Latin)
auratus = golden (from the Latin)

Thus we have the middle-sized golden hamster. In 1941, one hundred and two years after Waterhouse, Ellerman pointed out the *Mesocricetus* is actually a distinct genus, and so our hamsters' name since 1941 has been somewhat more properly called *Mesocricetus auratus auratus*.

In the tree of life one way to locate the golden Teddy Bear hamster is roughly as follows:

PHYLUM	*Chordata*	with a spinal cord
CLASS	*Mammalia*	nurse young
SUBCLASS	*Eutheria*	with placenta
COHORT	*Glires*	resembling the dormouse
ORDER	*Rodentia*	chisel-like front teeth
SUBORDER	*Myomorpha*	rats, mice and their allies
SUBORDER	*Simplicidentata*	one pair of upper chisel teeth—this eliminates the rabbits
SUPERFAMILY	*Muroidea*	mouse-like burrowing animals with some technicalities concerning their teeth which set them apart
FAMILY	*Cricetidae*	hamsters and voles
SUBFAMILY	*Cricetinae*	hamsters and their allies
SUBFAMILY	*Sigmodontinae*	this is a classification which really refers more to American white-footed mice, etc. (It is mentioned here simply because it appears in some of the older literature.)
TRIBE	*Cricetini*	hamsters (another technical division)
GENUS	*Mesocricetus*	middle-sized hamster
SPECIES	*auratus*	golden
SUBSPECIES	*auratus*	golden
VARIETY	*long hair*	Teddy Bear

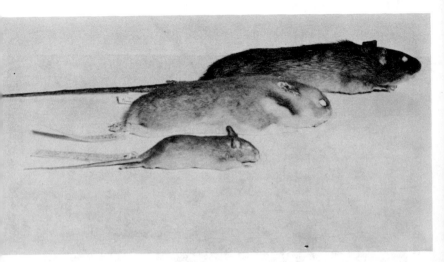

Stuffed skins of the rat (top), the hamster (center), and the mouse (lower) point up the hamster's short head and fullness of body.

Syrian hamster on the left, Chinese hamster in the center, and giant European hamster on the right.

Here for a quick comparison with the normal form of a hamster are three other popular rodent pets. Above are cavies, tailless rodents from Peru. Cavies are available in a number of colors and coat varieties.

Opposite, top: a gerbil, showing the typically hairy tail and mouselike body.

Opposite, lower photo: mice, showing typically dainty bodies and long, thin, tapering hairless tails.

CONVERSION OF WEIGHTS AND MEASURE

Unit of Measure	Equivalent
1 grain per gallon	17.12 parts per million
1 part per million	0.0584 grains per gallon
1 part per million	1 milligram per liter
1 gallon	231 cubic inches
1 cubic foot	7.48 gallons
1 cubic foot of water	62.4 pounds
1 gallon of water	8.34 pounds
1 gallon	3.785 liters
1 liter	0.2642 gallon
1 liter	1.057 quarts
1 liter	61.02 cubic inches
1 inch	2.54 centimeters
1 centimeter	0.3937 inch
1 gram	15.432 grains
1 kilogram	2.205 pounds
1 pound	7000 grains
1 pound	453.6 grams
1 meter	39.37 inches
1 cubic centimeter	0.0610 cubic inch
1 cubic inch	16.387 cubic centimeters
1 quart	0.046 liter
1 gram	0.0353 ounce
1 ounce	28.3495 grams
Fahrenheit Temperature	Centigrade Temperature $\times 1.8 + 32$
Centigrade Temperature	$\dfrac{\text{Fahrenheit Temperature} - 32}{1.8}$

NOTE: Fluid ounces, quarts and gallons are U.S. fluid measure and *not* British Imperial measure. One British Imperial gallon equals 1.2009 U.S. Gallons.

This hamster is being tamed by Martha Roberts, the author's daughter.

Home Measure (fluid)	U.S. Fluid Measure	Metric System
1 drop (eye dropper)	1/640 fl. oz.	1/20 c.c. (or ml.)
1 teaspoon	1/8 fl. oz.	4 c.c.
1 tablespoon	2/3 fl. oz.	20 c.c.
1 teacup	6 fl. oz.	180 c.c.
1 pint	16 fl. oz.	480 c.c.

Home Measure (Salt)	Weight (apoth.)	Metric Weight
1 level teaspoon	75 grains	5 grams
1 heaped teaspoon	125 grains	8 grams
1 level tablespoon	300 grains	20 grams
1 heaped tablespoon	500 grains	33 grams
1 teacup	7 oz.	220 grams

FEEDING DRUGS
To feed a 1 per cent level in food, add:
5.4 grams per lb. of food
0.2 ounces per lb. of food
83 grains per lb. of food

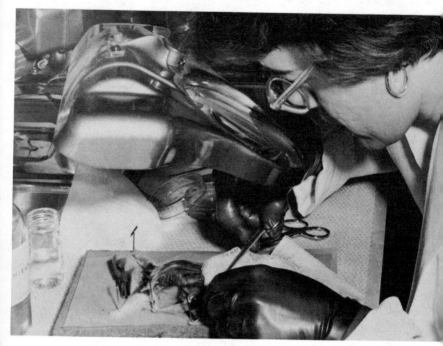

Hamsters are excellent animals for serious scientific research. Their cheek pouches are convenient for inplanting tissues, and their high rate of reproduction permits genetic studies of short duration. Here, above and right, Miss Alice Gale is shown at the Sloan-Kettering Laboratories in New York performing humanely designed surgical procedures on hamsters — hopefully to make our lives healthier, happier and longer.

3.

WHY THE HAMSTER
IS FAVORED

No one who has visited a pet shop can deny the popularity of the hamster, and the premium prices placed on Teddy Bear long hairs certainly attest to their

This man is a professional commercial hamster breeder who produces thousands of animals at a time. These animals are used for nutrition studies, food testing, scientific surgical medical research and genetic investigation in laboratories all over the world. Who knows but that you may be alive today because of what doctors have learned from their studies of processes in the hamster?

A comparison for size — a shorthaired golden hamster, (left) and a mouse. If left together, the hamster will kill the mouse.

desirability. Now, for the benefit of young people who wish to convince their "but you always say NO" parents, here is a short review of the qualities which make a hamster a desirable pet, and a Teddy Bear even more desirable.

It is a good size to hold in your hand, and when tamed and trained, it likes to be held. It is larger than a mouse and has a prettier face. And, it doesn't have the musky odor of a male mouse.

It is smaller than a rat and has a less prominent tail. In fact, a male Teddy Bear generally has his tail completely hidden by his long hair.

An old female Teddy Bear is being coaxed out of a box with a mix of seeds. She will probably stuff her pouches with only sunflower seeds and scurry back to her nearby cage.

A small metal cage with a wheel. This suffices for one hamster, but the bottom drawer will eventually rust or corrode from the hamster's urine.

It enjoys eating hoarded dry food, so it can be left over a weekend without a babysitter, so long as the watering bottle has been filled.

It can be kept in a smaller cage than a cavy (Guinea pig), and it doesn't wake you in the morning with its whistling.

It comes in more colors and hair patterns than a gerbil and is easier to breed if you wish to raise a few for your friends. And, it's larger than a gerbil which makes it more of a "cuddly" hand-holdable pet.

It has a unique cheek pouch arrangement where it can store up to half its body weight in food or bedding or something it wishes to steal. It is also unique in its ability to reproduce itself only sixteen days after mating. So, if you want a family, you need not wait nearly a month as you would if you had a rat, or over two months as you would if you had a cavy.

Cage security must keep cats out as well as hamsters in. Below is a typical metal cage with a wheel.

This sliding tray is great until it gets rusty. When it eventually jams, the bedding can be changed through the door.

Also, it lives only 1000 days maximum; so if you get tired of keeping hamsters, just stop breeding them and in less than three years, you will be free. In short, the Teddy Bear hamster is a fine pet for modest budgets, small quarters, simple equipment and intolerant older people.

Now that you have decided for hamsters, learn about them and enjoy them. It's easy.

The exercise wheel is especially important in a small cage.

4.

YOU AND YOUR PET

One hamster relates to you. Two hamsters relate to each other. For example, a female might kill a male if this is how she relates to him. If you are interested in a pet hamster, just keep one. The hamster variety you choose is like a necktie: you pay your money and take your choice. "Teddy Bears" are about the same weight as ordinary shorthairs, but they look larger. Male Teddy Bears tend to have longer hair than females. Male hamsters are often more even-tempered and friendly than females.

The short haired hamster shown here is tame, but the girl should not carry it on her shoulder, since a fall could kill it. Opposite, Neel F. Roberts is rushing the taming of a Teddy Bear, and he will soon be bitten.

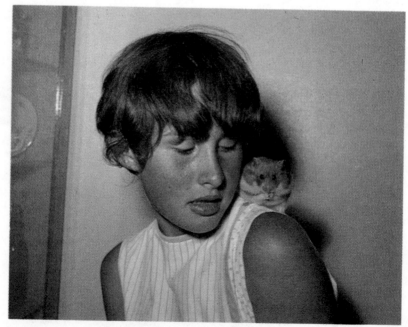

An old shorthaired male with dimorphic pigment spot just barely showing — see arrow.

Longhaired hamsters cost more than shorthairs. They may be a bit less prolific; this is a slightly educated guess, not a scientific statement of fact backed by statistics. Pink-eyed hamsters may have poorer vision than dark-eyed varieties. *Some* pink-eyed hamsters are known to be blind or nearly blind, but since most white hamsters are not pink-eyed but rather ruby-eyed, the problem is not as prevalent as one might suppose.

Long-haired hamsters seem to be just as gentle, intelligent, hardy and long-lived (1000 days) as short hairs.

Your long-haired pet hamster should come from a pet shop where the dealer knows his sources and where he can afford the time to keep young animals long enough to be sure they are healthy. A variety/discount type store is the worst place to buy a hamster. The help is usually inexperienced and their livestock is of the cheapest, lowest quality.

Choose a cub which weighs about 45 grams. A mature adult will weigh about 150 grams. The pet you choose should be lively, free from lumps and bumps (except, of course, his normal dimorphic pigment spots), his tail should be dry and ears erect and hairy. Hairless or shiny ears suggest an aged hamster. A healthy hamster has soft silky fur, a solid, plump body and prominent bright eyes.

A nick or hole in a hamster's ear is not a disease. It may be a breeder's mark or, more likely, it is as a result of a fight with another hamster.

The dimorphic pigment spots on the hips of the male seem to get relatively larger as he grows older. They may become as large in diameter as his eyes and as thick as two or three thicknesses of skin. Your pet may lick them in warm weather. This is all perfectly normal. When shopping for a pet hamster, watch out for a thin-faced long-tailed specimen. This is not a hamster, but more likely a mouse or a rat. Incidentally, hamsters must be kept apart from other animals. There is no reason to keep any other species of animal with your hamster and there are many reasons (mostly resulting in death) for not doing so.

These short haired cubs are just right for sale . . . weaned, but not too old.

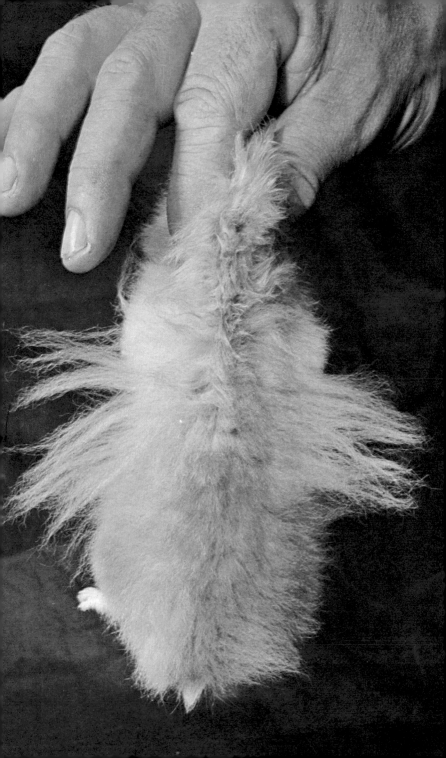

Belly (above) and dorsal (opposite) views of a young male Teddy Bear. He is sexually mature but may still grow another 20 grams or so. The hair is longest over his ribs.

5.

CHOOSING A PET HAMSTER

Hopefully you are reading this book *before* buying your first Teddy Bear. If this is not the case, read this chapter anyway, and when your breed your pet, aim for the features established in 1945 by British fanciers when they formed their first hamster club. Of course, the long hair came more than twenty-five years later, but the basic frame on which the hamster hangs his hair is still the same. Here then is the British Standard type:

The face on the larger animal (male) is longer than the standard desires.

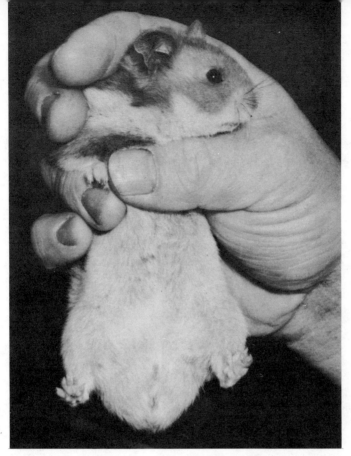

A mature male shorthair with the desired short face.

"The hamster shall be cobby, well-conditioned in body, with large head, broad skull, and short in face, blunt-nosed, avoiding all rat-like appearance. The head shall be well set in the body, as short necked as possible, with the general outline producing a smooth curve from the tip of the nose to the nape of the neck. The eyes shall be bold and prominent. The ears shall be set well apart, shall be large and of good width and shall be carried extended and alert when the animal is actively awake.

The animal shall be as large as possible, well fleshed and sturdy, but not fat."

This photo of a shorthair suggests the cobby features — sturdy and thick set. The stuffed pouches tend to emphasize the cobbiness. The Teddy Bear is harder to judge, since the longer hair masks these features.

A sexually mature young male Teddy Bear. Some specimens have longer hair on the rump as well as over the ribs.

So much for the standard. What it means to a pet keeper might take a little translating. For example, "cobby" means sturdy and thick-set. It is the opposite of slinky. The ideal hamster should be built like a grizzly bear and not like a Norway rat. The head should be as wide between centers of ears as from the nose to the top of the skull. The hamster should be large. The larger, the better, as long as the other features are not lost.

As this book goes to press, there is not enough known about the Teddy Bear to set a standard for its feature of long hair—possibly two standards, since some Teddy Bears seem to have rather straight hair while others exhibit a gentle wave. Not a kink or a curl, but certainly not straight.

6.

CAGING

Buy, don't build. Mr. Blandings built his dream house and proved the point that anything you can build can be bought for less, and it might very well be better. Remember, you will probably build a dozen or fewer hamster cages, but a hamster cage maker produces thousands and he probably worked out bugs *you* never thought of!

For production, try stainless steel or plastic boxes with screen $\frac{3}{8}''$ wire mesh covers. For a home hobby, consider an aquarium, or a birdcage, or a cage especially for small rodents available at your pet shop. Try for something strong and simple. Remember there must be an access for water. A water dish will not work as your hamster will quickly and deliberately fill it with bedding or feces. He is a desert animal—drinks drops of dew hanging from

A commercial breeder's nursery cage in use by Richard Smith of Stonehill Farms, Groton, Connecticut.

plants but standing water is foreign to *his* way of life. Don't try to change it—remember a hamster is a granivorous desert rodent—what little water he needs should be clean, fresh and dew like. The water access is best handled with a bottle, rubber stopper and glass tube—from above.

The cover should latch. Not gadgety—but simple and strong and easy to lock. Hamsters are escape artists, rivaled only by snakes, monkeys and parrots.

The cover might well provide ventilation. Remember the nest at the end of the burrow, eight winding feet long. If the cover is coarsely screened it will also be attractive to the hamster for exercise. He will climb about, upside down, for hours, every night. The wire will also get its share of gnawing which is nothing more than teeth sharpening and release of nervous tension. An exercise wheel is great if you can find room for it and don't mind the squeaking of the axle in the bearing all through the night. Never during the day—only at night! There may be a silent exercise wheel—find it if you can. Hamsters *do* need to exercise; if they don't, they are subject to paralysis.

Incidentally, studies have shown that a female is most active at that period in her oestrus cycle when she is receptive to breeding.

Weaned hamsters develop toilet habits with a little help from you. The urine is the problem, since the droppings tend to dry out quickly and dry droppings are virtually odorless. Here is where you can help:

(1) Avoid a wood bottom cage since the wood will soak up the urine and will always be damp and smelly. Plastic, glass or stainless steel are all good cage-bottom materials. Another reason for not recommending wood as a cage material is that it can be gnawed. If the wood is splintery and sharp it can hurt the hamster's mouth or cheek pouches. If it is thin, you may have an escape to contend with.

The breeder's cage with a female, her litter, a water bottle and a most important tag showing her past breeding history. The tag shows that she was first bred on December 5, but no pregnancy resulted. On January 3 she was bred again, and this time a litter of seven was produced on January 20 — and so on.

A Teddy Bear female and her litter of four. Note the soft fine texture of their fur, apparent even on the baby Teddy Bear hamsters.

(2) Provide plenty of bedding which your hamster can move around the cage. He will hide food in certain areas, build his nest elsewhere and sweep clean the spot where he leaves his liquid wastes. As they evaporate, you can scrape up the remainder and then blot up the last traces with a small wad of bedding which should then be thrown away.

Aspen wood shavings as used for bedding by Richard Smith of Stonehill Farms in Groton, Connecticut.

(3) Clean the cage often enough to keep the urine spot localized. If the *entire* cage is dirty or damp, the animal will have no cause to choose a particular spot to wet. How often? Once every week or two is a good point of departure. If you clean the cage too frequently, you will waste food and disturb his sense of security by ruining his nest and his hoard.

(4) Remember to clean the cage of a female *while* she is being mated. This technique will permit her to establish a nursery in anticipation of delivering a litter two weeks hence. Don't touch her cage contents again until the young are weaned. Since this whole process will take a month or so, it will be a good idea to provide extra bedding in this instance.

Bedding can be nearly anything which is not poisonous, overly aromatic, sharp or entangling. Paper confetti, wood chips, sawdust, shavings, mowed hay, chopped hay, cotton waste, have all been used successfully. Mr. Richard Smith of Stonehill Farms, Groton, Connecticut buys aspen wood shavings, even though he could get for free all the hay or sawdust he could possibly use. Aspen is also called poplar and is a soft wood—it is not aromatic like cedar, nor is it full of pitch like some of the pines. Two heaping handfuls provide a two-week supply for an adult of several youngsters together in a cage. The Teddy Bear's hair may get a little tangled in his wood shavings, but with a dry toothbrush, you can eliminate the tangles before they become a problem.

Escapes are a problem several ways. New Mexico has a climate like Syria—you have no business establishing an exotic rodent where he might take over from resident species. Another problem is that an escaped hamster might pick up parasites, ticks, fleas or disease and then when you capture him and put him back in the colony, you have introduced a Pandora's box. Still another is the possibility of loss to a predator; a dog, cat or a rat will quickly learn where the fun can be found and then watch out!

If a hamster escapes, you might try a live trap—there are many in the marketplace. Most are tunnel shaped with one or two doors at the ends and a treadle in the center. They work. Bait the treadle with something sticky—like peanut butter and with some grain pressed into it.

On these two pages are four examples of cages for pet hamsters. All provide the necessities; bedding, water, exercise wheel and security from cats.

This is about the smallest cage you should use for a single pet hamster.

Another technique is the apple-core-in-the-waste-basket gambit. Do just that, and provide a ramp up the outside. As long as the inside of the container is deeper than 10 inches and smooth, you have a trap. If you lose a male, put a receptive female in the trap. If she isn't receptive, put her in a small cage within the trap so that she cannot kill the poor fool after he falls in.

If your watering system is working reliably, you may leave your animals unattended for a weekend with little risk. Hedge your bet with a piece of raw potato or apple for extra moisture and be sure there is a plentiful supply of grain and dog biscuits in the cage. Incidentally, many experienced animal keepers supplement the diets of virtually all domestic and captive mammals with dried dog rations. This can be in biscuit or kibble form. The advantages of dry dog food are that trace elements are guaranteed available and spoilage is hardly ever a problem.

One accessory for the cage is a plastic, glass or metal scoop. It should be a little larger than your largest hamster. Use it to transfer a female to the cage of the male for breeding. There are two good reasons for this. First, there is less chance of your being bitten. Remember your hand is hamster size and it is invading another hamster's castle. Second, a female should smell like a female; conversely, she should not smell like your hand when she is introduced to the male. Perhaps your scoop can be a kitchen utensil, the kind some cooks use for dipping into flour or sugar. Another way to create a handy scoop is by cutting off the bottom and part of one side of a plastic bottle.

When you clean cages, don't use insect sprays or dusts since some may be dangerous to your animals, and if you provide 100% fresh clean bedding, the insects and insect eggs will be kept under control or entirely eliminated without the need for insecticides. This is not really a problem if you keep fewer than a hundred animals

Pick up a female hamster in a scoop or cardboard box or plastic jar if you plan to transfer her for mating.

This Teddy Bear is rather long-faced for the standard, but the texture of the hair is such a redeeming feature that the animal is worth keeping as a breeder.

Breathing into a nest box is a "no-no" while the litter is still blind or if you have a cold.

Hamsters, whether Teddy Bears or shorthairs, are curious and playful, and the cage in which they are maintained should allow them to display the traits that owners will most enjoy watching. Shown on this page and opposite are different arrangements, ranging from very simple to more elaborate, of the "Habitrail" hamster caging apparatus. Illustrations provided courtesy of the Metaframe Corp.

and don't introduce new stock directly "off-the-street."

If you expect to introduce additional hamsters to your stock, one or two cages should be kept empty and apart—in another room if possible—as quarantine for new or sick animals.

As a hamster ages, the hair on its ears has a tendency to be worn off, and in many cases hamsters (whether Teddy Bear or short-haired) exhibiting hairless "shiny" ears are older animals past their prime for breeding purposes.

Of all of the rodents that are kept as pets, the one that most close-
ly approaches the Teddy Bear as far as the length and softness
of the fur is concerned is the chinchilla. Photo by H. Hansen.

Here is an exercise wheel of novel design. It works just fine.

The Metaframe Mattel Living World people have introduced onto the pet market a popular unit they call "HABITRAIL." This is a well-conceived and well-manufactured expandable home, playground, gymnasium and easy-to-clean unit which is best explained when you see it.

7.

FEEDING HAMSTERS

Look at the hamster's four front teeth. He can gnaw, and open seeds and nuts. His rear teeth are harder for you to find, but with them he can crush the small things he gnaws. His *natural* food is mostly seeds, grain and hard dry desert vegetation. He drinks water but doesn't need much.

Like most of us, he has his preferences and his dislikes, too. A list of his first three preferences might go something like this: (1) sunflower seeds, (2) sunflower seeds, (3) sunflower seeds!! Actually, a dry mixture of cracked or whole corn, kibbled dog food, dog biscuits, sunflower seeds, wheat, and peas or beans is hard to beat. Supplement it with small fresh portions of newly mowed clover or hay, vegetables such as carrot, lettuce, potato—the less highly flavored varieties seem to be favored. Given a

A typical hamster food mix of sunflower seeds, corn, oats, wheat and dog biscuit.

Hamster pouch stuffing is normal and healthy so long as the material can be easily unstuffed by the animal. Sunflower seeds and kernels of whole corn are favorite items. The old male short-hair shown in these photos has prominent dimorphic pigment spots on his hips; the spots can be seen readily in two of the pictures. A Teddy Bear has the same spots, but his longer hair masks them. Photos by the author.

choice, most hamsters prefer apple over orange; lettuce over cabbage.

Soft foods should be fed carefully—thoughtfully. There is always a possibility that soft food may lodge in the cheek pouch where it could spoil and cause infection or other disease.

Sharp foods such as whole oats are also thought by some to be unsafe in the cheek pouch. Fortunately, most unsafe or unwholesome foods will be rejected by your pet and that will be the end of that.

Stale bread is often moistened with Pasteurized or evaporated milk as a diet supplement for expectant and nursing mothers and also for the young as they begin to stir from the nest. Feed only as much as they will clean up promptly. This is a food to be eaten, not stored. Hamster—the hoarder, remember?

Young hamsters and breeding females do well if offered supplemental treats like boiled eggs, live crickets, grasshoppers, lean meat, wheat germ, and mixed birdseed (containing millet and rape seed.)

Another excellent addition to the hamster's diet is a compressed, hard dry pelletized plant food available through your pet dealer. It comes in lumps about one inch in diameter and possibly an inch or two long. This is a mixture of freshly mowed clover alfalfa and timothy hay which has been chopped and extruded and dried. It keeps indefinitely if dry and hamsters bedded in anything but hay, should have it as a diet supplement.

Of course, if you have just one or two animals, your best source of food supply is your pet dealer who has packaged mixtures designed for hamsters. All you need to add is a watering bottle and occasional soft fresh treats like crickets, carrot, apple or a little lettuce. A *little* lettuce. Lettuce is a delicacy which is actually much more moist than most hamsters can tolerate in large quantities. It might lead to diarrhaea in some animals, if overfed.

A handful of dry pelletized plant food in compressed form; this material often is referred to as lab pellets.

Corn can be one of the staple grains in a hamster's diet.

8.
CHILDREN AND HAMSTERS

With intelligent leadership by patient adults, hamsters are great pets for children. Small enough to cuddle, large enough to focus attention upon, the Teddy Bear is a good first pet *with adequate supervision.*

Teach the child not to reach into the cage, but rather to let the hamster crawl out by himself. Teach the methods of holding without squeezing. Teach humane care and thoughtful loving attention—it should pay dividends for the rest of the child's life; certainly for the life of the hamster.

A well made cage keeps children out as well as pets in. The one shown here should *not* have the tower cover removed.

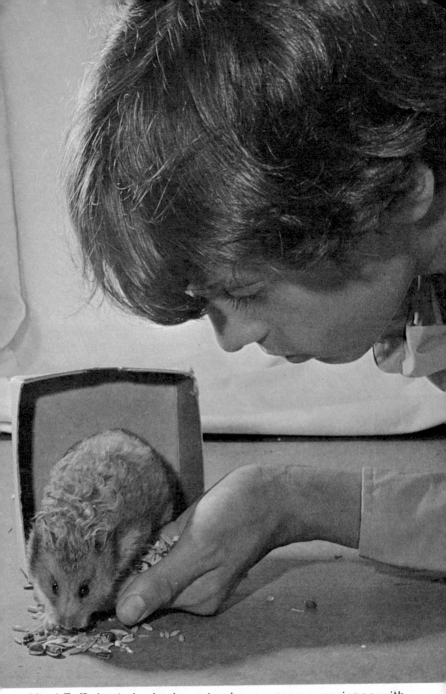

Neel F. Roberts is sharing a taming process experience with his pet Teddy Bear. This old male is quite "curly" coated.

9.

GROOMING AND BATHING

Teddy Bears may need brushing, gently please, with a toothbrush. Their teeth and nails generally wear down as they grow and need no attention. Bathing is required only for mange cures and reference to bathing is suggested in the chapter on **Diseases.** There is no reason to bathe a healthy hamster; he will groom himself clean as long as he is healthy.

A hamster whose ears were bitten during mating may be treated with an antiseptic like Mercurochrome or, better still, left to heal without medication.

10.

BREEDING

Don't try to remake hamster habits, but rather, adapt your techniques and equipment to suit what they do naturally. Hamsters are tunnel dwellers, they mate in the dark and are born in the dark and develop for several weeks, still in a dark nest at the end of a winding burrow, possibly eight feet long.

Most surface activity is probably at night. This is when they meet and mate. Since the nest at the end of the burrow is the nursery, the place of safety and food storage, it is defended against all comers. The female in her nest might well kill a visiting male. So, when you mate your animals, place the *female* in the cage of the *male*. He is more interested in her than in hoarding food, or protecting a nest of babies, and the chances of a successful mating without bloodshed are increased.

When the females are receptive to mating, they are more active than usual. This happens every fourth day, or more properly, every fourth or fifth night. A waxy plug develops in the opening of the vagina and it is discharged at the end of each cycle. The female is receptive to breeding at the beginning of a cycle, that is to say, when there is no discharge. This examination technique may be of value to scientists working on special problems, but for breeders of pet hamsters, it is not recommended simply because there is an easier method.

Sometime after 7 p.m. and before 11 p.m., place an active female in the cage of a large experienced male. Within a minute he will have sniffed and begun to mate with her if she is receptive. She will raise her tail and arch her back and stand still. Within thirty minutes the deed will have been done.

A female pink-eared white Teddy Bear going away shows the extra-long hair tufts at pouch, ribs and rump. On a male they would be even longer.

This golden Teddy Bear is lifted gently by the scruff of her loose neck skin for a quick examination before mating. She is perfect.

Don't leave them together overnight. She will not produce a bigger litter, but she may exhaust or hurt her mate before morning. He may stop or slow down to preen himself; this is normal. She may begin to fill her pouches with food from his hoard. This is normal too, but is a waste of your time. Try to keep the food in his cage at a bare minimum while he is providing stud service.

She may scuffle with him a little; this too is normal even for a receptive female, but if a fight develops, separate them immediately. Then, 24 hours later, try again. With this method one male can serve as many as ten breeding females with no strain on him. Remember these simple basic procedures:

1. Use an experienced male for assured production.
2. Try a female for a few minutes and remove her promptly if she is not receptive.
3. Keep a pair together no longer than 30 minutes.
4. Repeat the routine every night at the same time until she is receptive.

This baby hamster has had his eyes open for just one day. The ruler is for size comparison.

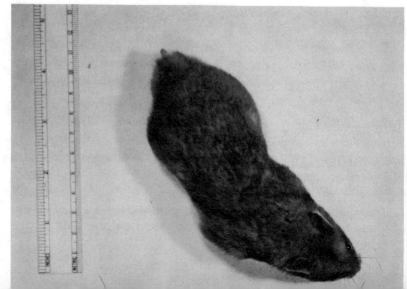

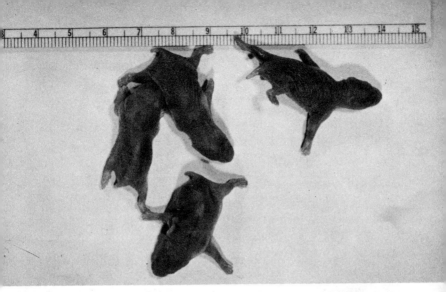

Just a few days old, these little fellows should not be kept from their mother for more than a minute. Still better, don't touch.

5. Keep trying the male only until you find a receptive female, then let them mate for 30 minutes; then don't use him again for 24 hours.

6. Once a female begins to mate, clean her cage during those 30 minutes. Fill it with extra bedding and extra food and plan for a litter in two weeks. Leave her strictly alone for 19 days and nights. If she does not deliver, try the mating technique again, *by the numbers*.

No matter how young your female is, somebody has probably bred one even younger. This is a meaningless exercise in diminishing returns. A female should be fully grown if you are to get any kind of production out of her. Litters from very young females are small, often weak, frequently born dead, and more often than not, they are killed and/or eaten. The female Teddy Bear hamster, under *normal* conditions, eats her dead or dying young as a sanitary measure.

Plan to breed a female only when she is at least eight or ten weeks old. She will probably be even better if she were twelve weeks old. Try to use an older, experienced male, the first time, anyway.

Keep records. Discard breeders which consistently produce malformed young. Leave pregnant females and females with young strictly alone. Pick up your animals in a box, can, jar or scoop. Don't handle them when transferring animals to cages for mating—your odor may confuse the issue. Avoid picking up the young, especially before their eyes open. If you must pick them up, rub a handful of grain over your hands first. It will tend to mask your odor. The babies photographed for this book were handled without loss, but the females were experienced mothers and the hand-rubbing technique was used.

A young male golden Teddy Bear from the rear displays his long rib and rump hair.

A Teddy Bear female and her four-day-old litter of seven. The bedding is aspen shaving. The nest is soft dry grass. The bedding is clean and dry. All these cubs grew up to healthy adulthood.

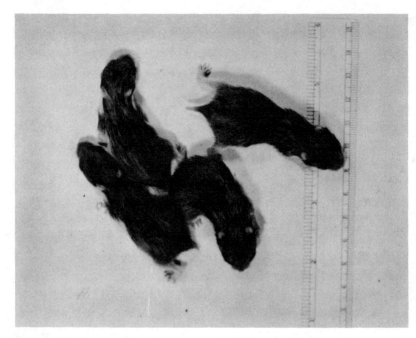

Hamster cubs about eight days old. They creep and even eat a little, but they cannot yet see.

Litters of normal, short-haired hamsters will range to twelve with an average of six. Still-births, runts and deformities might account for 2%. If your animals have a defect rate of 10%, you ought to find out why. Teddy Bears are somewhat harder to produce than normal short-haired strains. Litters are smaller and less frequent. Possibly their long hair interferes with mating.

Most female hamsters will produce about six or seven successful litters averaging six or seven cubs per litter in a lifetime. It doesn't matter seem to if you start at age 12 weeks or at 20 weeks for the first litter; a female fizzles out after forty or fifty offspring. If you have a strain which does better, keep them and concentrate on this genetic feature.

11.

RAISING
YOUNG HAMSTERS

Hamsters have raised hamsters for centuries with no help from us. If we insist on helping, we must do it passively. Provide the female with plenty of bedding, privacy and ample food for hoarding and eating. The water supply must be available to the babies even when their eyes are barely open. Many young hamsters die of thirst when they are weaned because the water bottle tube is so high they cannot reach it.

Soft foods, bread and milk, lettuce, meat, hard-boiled eggs are all good for babies—they will eat soft, moist bread three or four days before their eyes are fully open. They will even pack their tiny cheek pouches while their eyes are not open!

Don't help the mother gather her new litter as they are born. She will do it by herself after the last cub arrives. Keep the cages cool, dry, out of drafts, free from spoiling food, and protected from vermin, dogs, cats and little children. Keep the cage out of direct sunlight.

The babies should be sexed and separated after they stop nursing so that they cannot breed while too young. They might try when only four weeks old, but here is the point in time when you should make your presence felt.

If the mother kills her babies, it may be because you made her nervous or did not adequately shield her from some other irritant. If the mother eats her babies, it may be because she and they are under-nourished, i.e., underfed. If she kills them but does not eat them, it may be because she is poorly nourished, i.e., lacking a mineral or a vitamin.

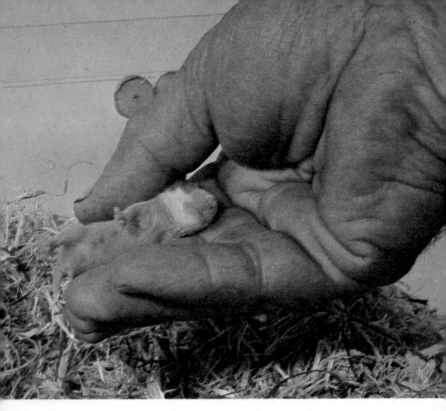

Above, a six-day-old female. Note the line of teats.

Young females who fail with their first litter often mature to become steady heavy producers of high quality young. The best productivity seems to come from females in the third through tenth months.

Hamsters are expected to live only 1000 days, and with a four day rhythm for ovulation and a two week period of gestation, the hamster has a short intense life. If you want production, you must utilize their time efficiently. Don't let them waste it in hibernation, aestivation or malnutrition.

A litter with two colors. Several are white and several are golden.

When you raise young hamsters, give them room to grow, fresh food, including greens and animal protein, convenient clean water and cool dry bedding. The emphasis on cool is because an overly warm hamster will aestivate— a deep, sleep-like hibernation which is so deep you might well assume your animal is dead and dispose of him. This aestivation is nature's way of carrying a furry animal over a hot period in a dry desert environment. How hot? Over 80° F. is aestivating temperature. Nights are cool, the hamster needs fur for his evening outdoor activity, but the hot, dry midday or hot, dry season with no rain and

A young male shorthair. His ears are hairy, denoting youth. His testicles are formed, so he is sexually mature.

no juicy fruits for liquid, will induce aestivation. To get your animal out of this state, circulate cool air and reduce the light.

When you raise hamsters in cool or cold places, they may hibernate. Same idea. To bring back activity, raise the temperature above 50° F. but below 70° F., and increase the amount of light, especially sunlight, if possible.

As you raise your hamsters, you may want to keep track of their growth. Use a 500 gram capacity beam balance and a scoop or small cardboard box to load the animal onto the balance. If the scoop has a round-number weight, say

```
┌──────────────────────────────────────────────────────────┐
│                                                          │
│  SIRE: No. 14              DAM: No. 23                    │
│    Agouti, long haired 1/1     Cream, banded: e/e Ba/—    │
│                                                          │
│  Litter #10:               Litter #11:                   │
│                                                          │
│      — 71 agouti               — 92 agouti               │
│                                                          │
│      — 72 agouti               — 93 agouti               │
│                                                          │
│      — 73 agouti                                         │
│                                                          │
│      — 74 agouti                                         │
│                                                          │
│      — 75 agouti                                         │
│                                                          │
└──────────────────────────────────────────────────────────┘
```

This is the type of record card which you might use to record the breeding data.

50 or 100 grams, subtraction will be easier. A full-grown normal golden short-haired hamster will weigh about 150 grams. One outstanding feature of the Teddy Bear is his size. Practically everyone who sees or handles them is bound to remark on their great size and weight. Here is where the scale is useful. Measurements of the adult Stonehill Farms animals used for Mr. Hall's pictures in this book showed them to range in weight between 140 and 154 grams. If there is any difference in weight between short hairs and long hairs, I have yet to discover it.

At the end of 1000 days of raising your hamster, he will be cancerous, mangy, rheumatic, or just too decrepit to even eat properly. Take him to your veterinarian and have him humanely and painlessly put to sleep.

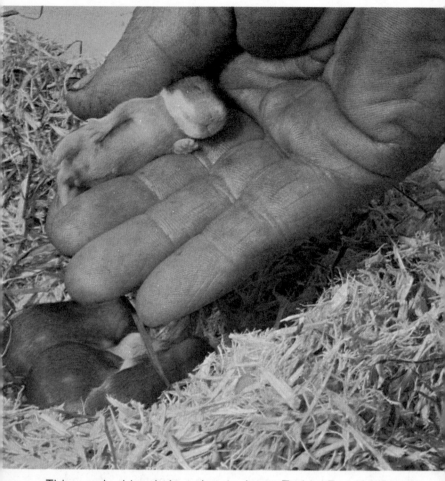

This week-old cub is going to be a Teddy Bear with wild type color and pattern.

These week-old cubs will surely be wild type in color and pattern, but the long hair feature is not yet apparent.

12.

GENETICS

This chapter was written by Dr. C. William Nixon of Randolph, Mass. Dr. Nixon has authored more than twenty scientific papers dealing with the genetics of the golden hamster. He has also published extensively on dog and plant genetics.

The so-called wild-type golden hamster is the "standard" from which the several variations deviate. Among the deviations from "normal" or wild-type is that of the long hair. Of course, long hair makes the "Teddy Bear."

The wild-type Syrian hamster has short hair of the color known as "agouti." This type of coloration, which incidentally is also characteristic of many of our wild animals, is practically indescribable since it varies in shading according to many factors such as lighting, stage of growth, etc. The reason for this fluctuation of color is due to the peculiarity of agouti hair which is that each hair is banded by several different colors from root to apex. If you part the fur of an agouti hamster, for instance, by blowing into it, you can easily see that the base of the hairs is of a dark blue-black color. The middle portion of the hair is brownish or golden which gives the animal the general golden color we see. The pointed tips of most of the hairs are black. Therefore, there are at least three distinct color bands in the agouti hamster fur. Belly fur of the agouti wild-type hamster is of a medium to light gray usually with some irregular white patches.

Over the years in captivity, since 1930, quite a few mutations from normal or wild-type fur have occurred, and these have been perpetuated in most cases as separate lines by scientists (if the mutation had some scientific

This is the basic building block — a wild type shorthaired hamster.

value), or by the pet trade (if the mutation was of some value to that industry in creating an attractive new type). The types of changes which may affect fur fall into three categories: (1) changes which affect overall hair color; (2) changes which affect the color pattern; (3) changes which affect the quality of the hair. The long-haired hamster falls into this third category.

You will note that, as a geneticist, *I* call the subject of this book "long-haired" rather than "Teddy Bear." In many respects, it is unfortunate that the term "Teddy Bear" was used in the first place as the name for this hamster variant. For example, who knows whether or not the long-haired hamster is at present or always will be the one which most nearly resembles a Teddy Bear? I can think of at least one other candidate for this similarity— a rare but closely-related species to the golden hamster, that in my opinion is far more Teddy Bear-like than the long-haired hamster. The term "long-haired" is a preferable one in that it is consistent with the same type of change in hair type that has occurred in other furred animals.

Another term in general usage for long hair type is "Angora." Thus we have long-haired dogs, cats, and rabbits, the latter two of which are also known as Angora. And now, of course, we have the long-haired hamster. It is the pet industry which has given the name "Teddy Bear" to this hamster, whereas the more precise and scientifically correct name is "long-haired."

There are several other known hair type mutations in the hamster which may be of passing interest to the reader, and all of them have counterparts in other animals. There are rex coated hamsters where the hair is kinky, and there are rex cats and rabbits; there are satin coated hamsters as well as rabbits; and finally, there are hairless hamsters in addition to cats, dogs, rats, mice, etc. Overall, however, mutations for coat type are fewer in number than are those for either hair color or pattern.

Most of the hair over the back of a normal coated hamster measures 10–15 mm in length, whereas that on the long-haired hamster measures 15–25 mm and may get as long as 65 mm, perhaps even longer near the rear of the animal. To be sure, there is a great deal of variation in hair length on the same hamster and also variation among long-haired hamsters. Present data from breeding these animals indicate that the gene for normal fur length in the hamster has mutated to one for long hair and furthermore that it is a simple recessive mutation.

The symbol "l" (for "long hair") has been given to this factor. Normal short hair is dominant and it is designated by the symbol "L". Results of breeding these hamsters also indicate that there may be modifying factors that cause variations in the length of the long hair. If such modifiers are indeed present, then it would be advantageous

This is a big old female golden Teddy Bear. Her hair is long-est behind her ears. The hair on her male offspring is twice as long nearly everywhere.

A piebald shorthair. In less than a year this strain could be established in the Teddy Bear — theoretically.

to select those long-haired specimens having the greatest fur length for breeding.

(a) long hair (**1/1** x long hair (**1/1**)=100% long hair (**1/1**, homozygous)

(b) long hair (**1/1**) x short hair (**L/L**, homozygous)=100% short hair (**L/1**, heterozygous)

(c) short hair (**L/1**, heterozygous) x short hair (**L/1**, heterozygous)=75% short hair (**L/L** and **L/1** mixed) and 25% long hair (**1/1**)

(d) short hair (**L/1**, heterozygous) x long hair (**1/1**)=50% short hair (**L/1**, heterozygous) and 50% long hair (**1/1**)

(e) short hair (**L/1**, heterozygous) x short hair (**L/L**, homozygous)=100% short hair (50% of which are homozygous, **L/L**, and 50% of which are heterozygous, **L/1**).

The preceding formulae with their ratios are the *chances* of things happening. The results one may actually get in a single litter (or even two or three litters) may deviate considerably from those one should get in theory. The so-called "perfect ratio" (that is, when the results of breeding are the same as those of the theoretically perfect ratio) is usually approached only when several hundred offspring of a given type of cross are added together. You consider yourself lucky if you get such a ratio in a single litter.

There are many interesting combinations that can be made between long hair type and the various colors and patterns already in existence. These combinations provide sufficient challenge to satisfy the hobbyist, as well as the budding scientist in school, who is searching for a research project. For those who may wish to delve into the more technical aspects of hamster color genetics, see:—C. William Nixon, John H. Beaumont, and Maureen E. Connelly: Gene Interaction of Coat Patterns and Colors in the Syrian Hamster. Journal of Heredity **61** (5): 221–228; Sept.-Oct., 1970.

Long-haired hamsters of various colors have already been produced by the pet industry. Some of these are black-eared, white, pink-eared white, and cream. However, many others have not as yet been produced. Included are the infinite number of possibilities for various combinations of colors with other colors, colors with patterns, and patterns with other patterns, nearly all of which should be possible to obtain together with long hair.

Let us list the possible basic colors and patterns from which one can work to create something new and different. Attention should be paid to the fact that at the time of this printing, the hamster has *never* mutated to a complete and true albino. The mutation for white fur with black ears and dark red eyes in the adult is apparently in the albino series but is not a complete albino, which would have no pigment or genes for pigment at all. The black-eared white hamster is called acromelanic white and is symbolized by **cd**. Therefore, a **cd/cd** animal is of this color. It is possible in addition, to produce a pseudo-albino by combining **cd/cd** with brown **b/b**, another mutation for reduction of pigment. The resulting animal (**cd/cd b/b**) mimics the true albino in that little or no pigment is present, and it is called pseudo-albino. This is a pink-eyed, pink-eared white variety and it *looks* like an albino. A true albino, *if* such occurred, would be **ca/ca**, since **ca** represents the most extreme and complete form of albinism in the series and one where no pigment is formed, whereas **cd** is one of the several possible mutants for *partial* albinism in the albino series.

Albinism, when it occurs, is a recessive genetic factor. Here then, is a list of some interesting colors and patterns in hamsters. There are literally thousands of possible combinations of these factors with long hair, so that one is limited only by the imagination, and the reward is the satisfaction of having created something different.

Pattern Factors

(1) PIEBALD (**s**) is a form of recessive white spotting It is sometimes called "pied", "harlequin", or "panda." The **s/s** animal has irregular white patches of fur scattered throughout whatever basic color the hamster may be. A white blaze on the forehead is often present and usually indicates the **s/s** combination. In addition to white spotting, the **s/s** animal is smaller and less vigorous than its non-spotted relatives, a good example of the multiple effects of a gene.

(2) WHITE BAND (**Ba**). This dominant pattern factor causes the animal to have a white band completely or almost completely encircling the trunk and thereby interrupting the basic color of the animal. Its width

A pink-eared, pink-eyed white female Teddy Bear and her ruby-eyed cub.

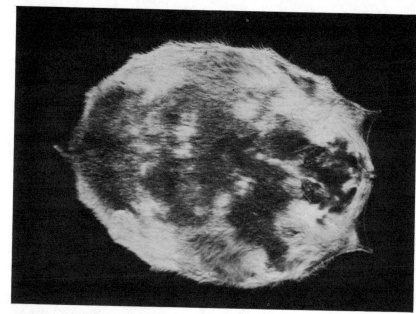

On this page and opposite are dorsal views of the pelts of Teddy Bear hamsters showing different patterns of markings.

Above is a piebald (s/s) and below a white band (Ba.) Photos by Dr. C. W. Nixon.

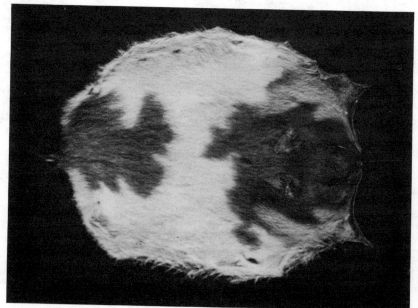

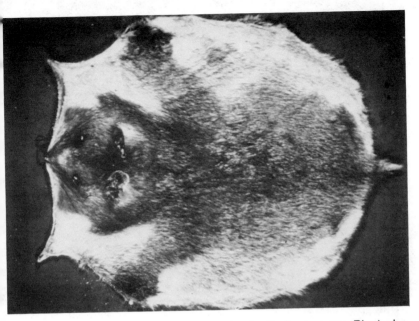

Wild type (agouti) pattern. Here the belly fur is gray. Photo by Dr. C.W. Nixon.

Heterozygous anophthalmic white (Wh/wh) pattern, popularly called "imperial." In this animal the belly fur is white. Photo by Dr. C. W. Nixon.

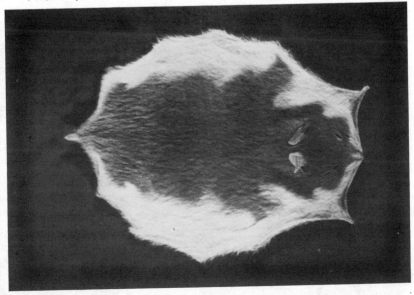

White band (Ba) of varying widths. This is a dominant factor. If either parent is banded, the offspring will be banded too.

Four degrees of spotting in piebald recessive white.

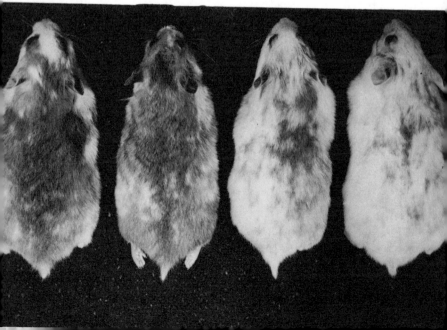

varies considerably and may be interrupted by a dorsal area of colored fur. White and colored areas do not intermingle, giving the animal a most striking appearance. In cases where the white band is broader than usual, it encroaches upon the shoulder and flank areas. Belly fur varies in color from almost totally gray when the band is minimal, to completely white when the band is large. The banded animal is undoubtedly one of the most attractive, especially when it is in combination with the darker colors. Since banding is a dominant factor, both heterozygous and homozygous animals have the band.

A young male with wild type color and pattern, but certainly a Teddy Bear.

(3) ANOPHTHALMIC WHITE (**Wh**). Homozygous (**Wh/Wh**) animals are called anophthalmic white or "blind albino." A better name for this mutant would be microphthalmic white, since the eyeballs are usually present but reduced in size in varying degrees. "*Microphthalmic*" means small eyes, whereas "*anophthalmic*" means no eyes. These animals have no pigment (white fur color and pink ears), and the eyes are either reduced or absent. When present, the eyes are pink. Rarely, homozygous animals are found that have almost normal sized eyeballs. When these apparently normal-eyed animals are bred to each other, they produce anophthalmic white young. Therefore, the parents are considered to be **Wh/Wh**. In this case, the **Wh/Wh** condition allows considerable variation in the degree of eye defects from near normal to almost total absence of eyeballs.

The heterozygous factor (**Wh/wh**) is popularly called "*imperial*" and causes the belly fur to be white instead of gray. A barely noticeable sprinkling of white guard hairs is distributed over otherwise normally pigmented dorsal portions of the animal.

Color Factors

(1) ACROMELANIC ALBINISM (**cd**). We have already discussed this factor in the preceding section and therefore need only mention that this is a recessive factor and that it is not a complete albino and should be called either by its correct name or by perhaps "black-eared white." At any rate, the fur is white, but dark pigment is present in the adult in the ears, the skin around the anus and genitalia, and the eyes which turn red with age. The weanling hamster of this type, however, may give every indication of being a complete albino, since the localized pig-

mented areas become so only as maturity is reached. This factor in combination with *recessive* brown (**b**) produces a pseudo-albino, thereby actually mimicking the true albino condition.

(2) CREAM or NON-EXTENSION OF EUMELANIN (**e**). This genetic color factor is recessive and causes the elimination of most of the dark pigment but leaves the yellowish pigment in the fur. Therefore, the dorsal fur of the **e/e** animal is one of the deeper shades of cream or yellow, and belly fur is paler yellow. The eyes are black. As the animal matures, the skin of the ears and around the anus and genitalia becomes black.

(3) RUST (**r**) and (4) BROWN (**b**). These are both recessive factors, causing normal wild-type agouti coloration to become a few shades lighter, resulting in a lighter orange-brown. Belly fur is a little lighter than it is in the normal agouti animal. The dorsal fur of the brown animal is a trifle lighter in its brown to orange coloration than that of the rust hamster, but the difference is so small that it takes a skillful eye to detect it. Therefore, it is important to note that in rust animals, the eye color is black and the rim of the eyelid is also darkly pigmented, since these are the most obvious differences between this factor and brown (**b**). The brown animal has dark red eyes with unpigmented eyelids. One must often rely on eye and eyelid color here in order to distinguish successfully between the two factors.

(5) LETHAL GRAY (**Lg**). This is a dominant genetic factor which has another peculiarity in addition to a change in coat color from brownish-orange agouti to dark gray agouti. The lethal gray animal is always heterozygous (**Lg/lg**), that is, it carries the normal gene. Apparently, the homozygous condition of lethal gray (**Lg/Lg**) is lethal at some early stage of development

so that a living specimen is never produced. The coat is basically light gray with a silvery undercoat and a slight yellow or orange overcast. Belly fur is light gray, and eyes and ears are black.

There are several other patterns and colors known in hamsters which have not been mentioned here, but these are generally unavailable at present and can well be the topic of a complete book on hamster genetics. However, by utilizing the eight factors described here in all possible combinations, it is possible to produce several hundred different color varieties of hamsters.

How does one go about getting a long-haired hamster which also exhibits one or more of the patterns and colors? It really is not difficult, but it will ordinarily require a minimum of two hamster generations. First, you must acquire a long-haired hamster of either sex. The animal of the opposite sex should be one showing the desired color, pattern, or both. The two are then mated to produce the first generation offspring (the F_1 generation). These youngsters will likely exhibit none of the traits you wish. The next step is to breed these F_1 animals together to produce as many F_2 young as possible, since it is here that you will get all possible combinations of factors that went into the first cross. With a little luck, you should be able to select a pair of the desired combination which, when mated to each other, should continue to produce and perpetuate that particular variety. Lethal gray ones, of course, will always produce approximately one-half of non-lethal gray offspring, even in the first generation since it is dominant, but that poses no serious problem since it is easy to select the ones desired for breeding in each generation.

It is well to remember that the dominant factors (lethal gray, white band, and anophthalmic white) will be evident in the first generation (F_1) offspring where you will be able

A young male with wild type color and pattern, but certainly a Teddy Bear

to select the ones for your breeding stock to produce the desired second generation. It is only at the second generation level that long-haired animals will occur in association with the colors and patterns you started with.

An alternative breeding plan would be that of breeding the F_1 animal back to its parent. This is called a back-cross and is of value only if the parents are still alive and productive. In hamsters, reproductive life begins early, proceeds rapidly, and tapers off at a rather young age. Therefore, it is conceivable that one or both parents might be beyond reproductive age (or even dead) by the time that their F_1 offspring are ready for breeding.

The conclusion of all this? The field is wide open, so get busy. It takes a little time and patience to do it, but the fun and interest generated are genuine and the price is negligible for value received. Besides, hamsters are fun. Good luck!

13.

GENETICS GLOSSARY

ACROMELANISM—the color pattern where darker pigmentation appears on the extremities of the body. The Siamese cat is an example of this.

ALLELE—alternative characters. Long hair versus short hair.

BACK-CROSS—the mating of a hybrid to one of its parents.

DOMINANT—a characteristic which results from either a single or double dose of a gene. This is contrasted to a recessive which is hidden unless both genes are alike.

EUMELANIN—melanin, a complex organic compound, is the pigment which is almost totally responsible for coat color. Melanin exists in two distinct forms: (*a*) eumelanin, which is of varying shades of brown—

black; and (b) phaeomelanin, which is of varying shades of yellow-red.

GENE—the unit of heredity which controls the development of a character. A character is also called a characteristic, like long hair or pink eyes.

GENOTYPE—the complete genetic makeup of an animal, not necessarily just what shows. The visible aspect is the phenotype. One example could be a "golden" short hair. This is a description of a phenotype, but one such individual could be recessive for long hair or white spots or ruby eyes.

HETEROZYGOUS—for a particular trait, one gene differs from its companion. See *dominant* and *recessive*.

HOMOZYGOUS—Both genes are alike throughout. This is the "pure" strain. There are no "hidden" recessives.

HYBRID—the offspring of parents who differ in one or more genes. Also refers to offspring from parents not of the same species. The classic example is the mule, derived from a male donkey (jackass) and a female horse (mare). Hybrids of differing species are usually sterile.

INBREEDING—mating of relatives. Brother-sister, cousins, father-daughter, etc. This will eventually result in establishing a pure breed.

LINKAGE—a tendency for some characteristics always to appear together on an individual. This happens when the genes for these characteristics are all on the same chromosomes.

MUTATION—a sudden genetic change.

PHENOTYPE—the appearance of an individual; as opposed to genotype which is its genetic constitution, not necessarily apparent.

RECESSIVE—a character which shows up only when both of a pair of genes are alike.

VARIATION—the differences within a species. For example, color, pattern and hair length.

Genetics Bibliography

Beher, Margaret E. and Beher, W. T. (1959). A partial dominant for suppression of color in the Syrian hamster *Cricetus, Mesocricetus auratus. Amer. Nat. 93*, 201.

Foote, C. L. (1949). A mutation in the golden hamster. *J. Hered. 40*, 101.

Foote, C. L. and Foote, F. M. (1950). A comparative study of normal and piebald hamsters. *Trans Ill. Acad. Sci. 43*, 237–243.

Magalhaes, Hulda (1954). Mottled-white, a sex-linked lethal mutation in the golden hamster, *Mesocricetus auratus*. (Abstract.) *Anat Rec. 120*, 752.

Nixon, C. W. (1964). Some anatomical characteristics of eight inbred strains of *Mesocricetus auratus auratus* (Syrian hamster). (With F. Homburger, J. R. Baker and R. Whitney. J. Genetics) (Belghoria, W. Bengal, India) *59*, 1–6.

Nixon, C. W. (1964). Rust, a new mutation in Syrian hamsters. (With R. Whitney and G. Burns). *The American Naturalist, 98*, (899): 121–122.

Nixon, C. W. (1967). Dark gray and Lethal gray—two new coat color mutations in Syrian hamsters. (With Maureen E. Connelly). *Journal of Heredity, 58*, (6): 295–296.

Nixon, C. W. (1969). Dominant spotting: A new mutation in the Syrian hamster. (With Rae Whitney, John H. Beaumont, and Maureen E. Connelly). *Journal of Heredity, 60*, (5): 299–300.

Nixon, C. W. (1970). Gene interaction of coat patterns and colors in the Syrian hamster. (With John H. Beaumont and Maureen E. Connelly). *Journal of Heredity, 61*, (5): 221–228.

Nixon, C. W. (In press) Rex Coat; a new mutation in the Syrian hamster. (With Rae Whitney) *Journal of Heredity*.

Robinson, R. (1955). Two new mutations in the Syrian hamster. *Nature, Lond. 176*, 353–354.

Robinson, R. (1957). Partial albinism in the Syrian hamster. *Nature, Lond. 180*, 443–444.

Robinson, R. (1958). Genetic studies of the Syrian hamster. I. The mutant genes cream, ruby-eye and piebald. *Genetics 56*, 1–18.

Robinson, R. (1959). Genetic independence of four mutants in the Syrian hamster. *Nature, Lond. 183*, 125–126.

Robinson, R. (1959). Genetic studies of the Syrian hamster. II. Partial albinism. *Heredity 13*, 165–177.

Robinson, R. (1960). Light undercolor in the Syrian hamster. *J. Hered. 60*, 111–115.

Robinson, R. (1960). Occurrence of a brown mutation in the Syrian hamster. *Nature, Lond. 187*, 170–171.

Robinson, R. (1960). White band, a new spotting mutation in the Syrian hamster. *Nature, Lond. 188*, 764–765.

Whitney, Rae (1958). Behavior of three coat-color factors in Syrian hamsters. *J. Hered. 49*, 181–184.

14.

DISEASES

Let's start out with a few basics and then get into the details. Basic number one is that hamsters are naturally hardy and naturally resistant to disease. Basic number two is that they are subject to the same *sort* of diseases that man is subject to, and for the same reasons. That is: injuries, nutritional diseases, infectious diseases. Basic number three is that hamsters respond to disease cures much as people do. In other words, some hamsters recover with care, some recover spontaneously, and others die regardless, just like people. So much for the basics.

This is a healthy shorthair. Its body is rounded, its ears are fully extended and its appetite is excellent.

Now for the details—and here it should be mentioned that this is a whole book of details. For instance, water is mentioned in the feeding and rearing chapters, and cage cleanliness is discussed in the chapters on caging and also breeding.

Detail number one is that the homily *"cleanliness is next to Godliness"* is true. Many diseases can be cured or prevented by using clean bedding and changing it before it becomes an invitation to vermin. Remember to disinfect the cage when you change the bedding. This is easy with glass or metal or plastic cages, but much more difficult with wood. Water bottles should also be kept clean and, of course, your pet should never be expected to drink water which you wouldn't drink.

The second detail is another homily *"you are what you eat."* Your pets should never get any more soft foods than they will EAT *immediately.* *"Eat"* is emphasized. Remember the cheek pouches and the hoarding instinct. Soft foods include meat, fruits, vegetables, cooked foods and milk products—everything except grains, kibbled foods, pellets and water. Your pets should have a surplus of hard grains to hoard. This is important for their mental health as well as their physical health. Remember, they forage during the cool night and probably eat from the hoard three cool feet underground during the heat of the day. Nutrition is simple if you let your pet decide. Start with the list in the chapter on feeding and supplement it with small portions

This young hamster hasn't caught up with its ears, but the dimorphic pigment spot on the hip (circled) appears as an area of thinned hair.

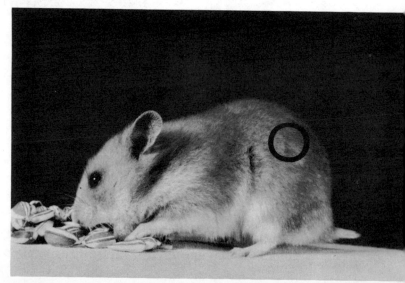

of whatever treats your pet enjoys.

The third detail considers injuries. Treat your pet with loving, thoughtful kindness. Don't try to remake him. He is not an acrobat or flier, or even much of a climber. Cage him and handle him with the view in mind that he must never fall. Also cage him so that he cannot escape and so no cat or dog or undisciplined child can get in to abuse him. Really, that is about all that there is to disease prevention.

Now, for CURES. Let's start with symptoms and then go into diagnosis and treatment.

Ruffled coat, loss of appetite, wasting, diarrhea, eventual death—this could be salmonellosis, an intestinal infection which can become epidemic. It may be transmitted by wild rodents or dirty drinking water or spoiled soft foods. Control and cure require that you destroy all sick animals. Isolate healthy animals, sterilize cages and equipment. Start anew with fresh bedding and a new food supply.

Ruffled coat, loss of appetite, rapid breathing, nasal discharge, coughing, sneezing, catarrh. This is an inflammation of the lungs—pneumonia, if you will. Again, as in salmonellosis—the same measures are suggested. Also, avoid sneezing at your pets; they may catch your cold. These respiratory diseases generally occur in malnourished colonies of damp and/or overcrowded animals.

Poor general condition, shakes head, scratches ears, loss of hair. Eventually, ears, nose, and genitals covered with gray warty scabs. The diagnosis is mange, caused by parasitic spiders or insects. The control is a high standard of hygiene. Wash your hands after handling each animal. Sterilize all cages and appliances. Replace all bedding. Avoid contact between infected and uninfected animals. There are mange cures available through your veterinarian. He can diagnose mange and possibly he will suggest a bath with benzyl benzoate, dimethyl-thianthrene or gammexane preparations.

Skin parasites are not common on pet hamsters, but if they do infest your colony, you have a problem. Read Chapter 9 entitled "Ectoparasites" in *Breeding Laboratory Animals* edited by G. Porter and W. Lane-Petter and published by T.F.H. Publications, Inc. Neptune City, New Jersey.

If the symptoms are poor general condition, diarrhea, and wet and dirty hind quarters, your pet has an infection called "wet tail." This is often fatal and can become epidemic. Wet tail is often a disease of neglect. Damp cages, spoiled food and malnourished animals are generally involved. The cure is doubtful—the control is obvious.

The runt will soon die. Its littermate might even eat it if it is left in the cage.